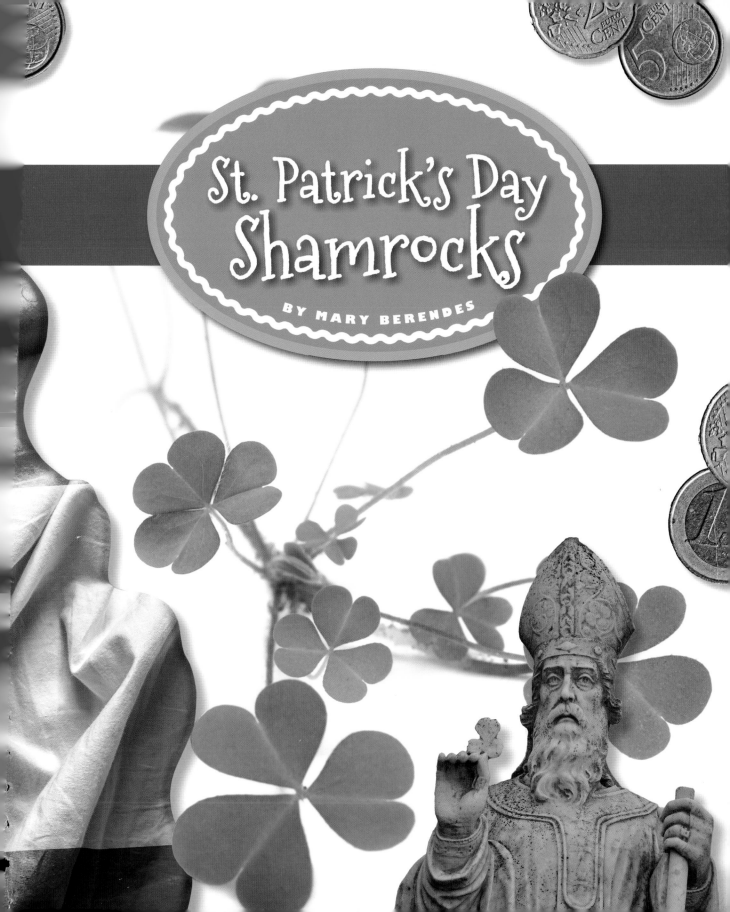

St. Patrick's Day
Shamrocks

BY MARY BERENDES

The Child's World®

Published by The Child's World®
1980 Lookout Drive • Mankato, MN 56003-1705
800-599-READ • www.childsworld.com

ACKNOWLEDGMENTS

The Child's World®: Mary Berendes, Publishing Director
The Design Lab: Design
Olivia Gregory: Editing
Pamela J. Mitsakos: Photo Research

Design elements ©: Filipe Frazao/Shutterstock.com: flag; M Reel/
Shutterstock.com: statue; Robcartorres/Shutterstock.com: euros
Photographs ©: Aduldej/Dreamstime.com: 11; bensueley/iStock.
com: 19; Bocman1973/Shutterstock.com:17; Evgeniya Uvarova/
Shutterstock.com: 5; GeoM/iStock.com: 7; Matt Ragen/Shut-
terstock.com: 15; pedrosala/Shutterstock.com: 9; seeingimages/
Dreamstime.com: 13; Swapan Photography/Shutterstock.com:
cover, 1; Terrie L. Zeller/Shutterstock.com: 21

ISBN 9781631437465
LCCN 2014945409

Printed in the United States of America
Mankato, MN
November, 2014
PA02244

Table of Contents

Meet the Shamrock!

Green decorations are everywhere on St. Patrick's Day. Look at them closely. You will see that many of the decorations are shaped like tiny green plants. Each of the leaves on these plants has three parts. The parts have round edges. What are these strange-looking plants? They're shamrocks!

Shamrocks grow together in large groups. They can cover an area of ground the same way grass does.

What Are Shamrocks?

Shamrocks are **trefoils** (TREE-foylz). That means their leaves have three parts. People are not exactly sure what kind of plant shamrocks are. Most agree that they are clover plants. Clover plants have very short **roots**. A plant's roots grow in the soil and soak up water.

Clovers have small, rounded leaves and short stems. These things make it easy to tell them apart from other plants.

7

Why Are Shamrocks Green?

Shamrocks are green. They get their color from something called **chlorophyll** (KLOR-uh-fill). Chlorophyll is in almost every part of a plant. It lets plants soak up energy from the sun. Plants use this energy to make food. This process is called **photosynthesis** (foh-toh-SIN-thuh-sis).

The chlorophyll in shamrocks makes them the perfect color for celebrating St. Patrick's Day!

What Is St. Patrick's Day?

St. Patrick's Day is a **holiday** that takes place every year on March 17. People spend the day celebrating the country of Ireland. They wear green clothes to remember the green fields of Ireland. They cook Irish food and listen to Irish music. Green shamrocks can be seen everywhere.

You don't have to be Irish to celebrate St. Patrick's Day. It is a lot of fun no matter where you're from!

Who Was St. Patrick?

St. Patrick was born long ago in Britain. He was kidnapped by pirates when he was 16 years old. The pirates sold him to work as a slave in Ireland.

Patrick was very unhappy and missed his family in Britain. He prayed that God would help him get free.

St. Patrick is an important **religious** figure. His image can be seen in statues, stained glass, and paintings throughout the world.

13

Patrick came back home to Britain after having a dream. In the dream, God told him about a ship he could use to escape. Soon, Patrick had another dream. He dreamed that God told him the people of Ireland needed him. Patrick went to study at a **monastery**. Then he sailed back to Ireland.

A carving of St. Patrick's head is on display at Chapel Royal in Ireland's Dublin Castle.

What Did
St. Patrick Do?

Patrick taught the Irish people about God. He **preached** to anyone who would listen. He helped build churches and schools. Soon, people everywhere began to hear about Patrick. They began telling stories about him. These **legends** are still known today.

There are many different stories about St. Patrick. That is one reason people still remember him today.

The Legend of St. Patrick and the Shamrock

The best-known legend about St. Patrick involves the shamrock. Patrick's teachers at the monastery told him that God was made of three beings. People in Ireland did not understand this idea. Patrick told the people that God's three parts were like the three parts of the shamrock's leaf.

The legend of
St. Patrick and the
shamrock is interesting,
but it is not
necessarily true.

Shamrocks Today

People today view shamrocks as lucky charms. The shamrock is also a **symbol** of Ireland. Its green color reminds people of Ireland's green countryside.

You might not believe the legend of St. Patrick and the shamrock. Shamrocks are still cute and colorful, though. They are fun to decorate with on St. Patrick's Day!

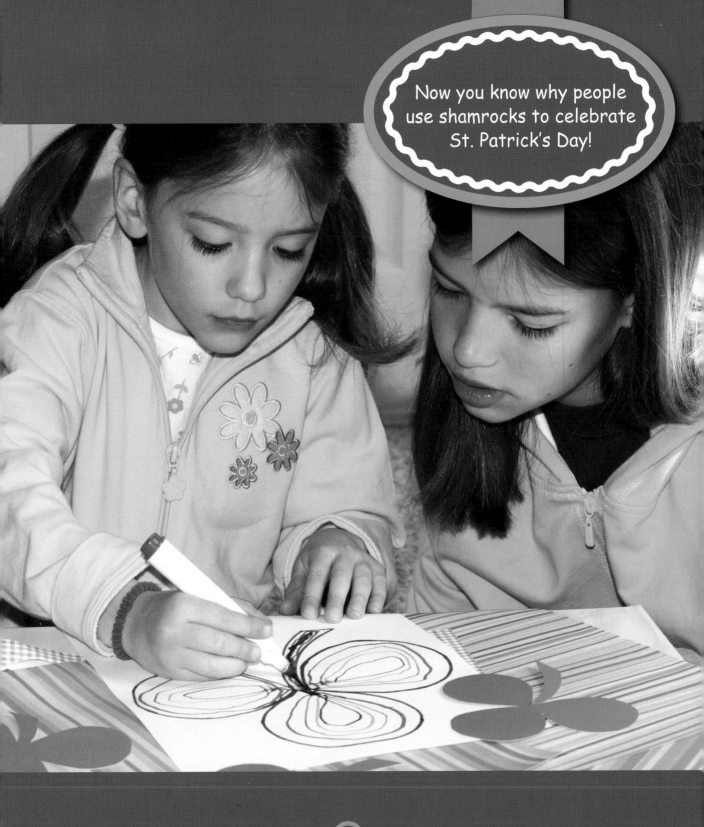

GLOSSARY

chlorophyll (KLOR-uh-fill) Chlorophyll is a green coloring found in most plants. It lets the plants soak up energy from the sun to make food.

holiday (HOL-uh-day) A holiday is a special day that people celebrate every year. St. Patrick's Day is a holiday.

legends (LEJ-uhndz) Legends are stories that are passed on from person to person. There are many legends about St. Patrick.

monastery (MON-uh-stayr-ee) A monastery is a place where people go to live and learn about God. St. Patrick learned about God in a monastery before he returned to Ireland.

photosynthesis (foh-toh-SIN-thuh-sis) Photosynthesis is the process that green plants use to make food. Shamrocks use photosynthesis.

preached (PREECHD) To preach is to tell a group of people about religious ideas.

religious (ruh-LIH-jus) When something is religious, it has to do with a religion, such as Christianity or Judaism.

roots (ROOTS) Roots are the parts of a plant that grow underground. Clover plants have short roots.

St. Patrick (SAYNT PA-trik) St. Patrick was a man who preached about God in Ireland more than 1,500 years ago.

symbol (SIM-bull) A symbol is an object that stands for something else. Shamrocks are a symbol of Ireland.

trefoils (TREE-foylz) Trefoils are plants that have leaves with three parts. Shamrocks are trefoils.

BOOKS AND WEB SITES

BOOKS

dePaola, Tomie. *Patrick, Patron Saint of Ireland.*
New York: Holiday House, 1992.

Gibbons, Gail. *St. Patrick's Day.* New York: Holiday House, 1994.

Mercer, Abbie. *Happy St. Patrick's Day.* New
York: PowerKids Press, 2008.

Roop, Peter and Connie. *Let's Celebrate St. Patrick's
Day.* Brookfield, CT: Milbrook Press, 2003.

WEB SITES

Visit our Web site for lots of links
about St. Patrick's Day shamrocks:
childsworld.com/links

*Note to Parents, Teachers, and Librarians:
We routinely verify our Web links
to make sure they are safe, active sites—
so encourage your readers to check them out!*

INDEX

ABOUT THE AUTHOR

Mary Berendes has authored dozens of books for children, including nature titles as well as books about various countries and holidays. A longtime resident of Minnesota, Mary has numerous pastimes, including collecting antique books and dabbling in photography, to occupy her during the long winters. Her beloved Yorkshire terrier also provides plenty of entertainment, confusion, and comic relief on a daily basis.